At "The Elite Dad", our mission is all about supporting and empowering families. We're here to motivate, inspire, educate, and equip you with all the tools you need to improve your lives and live your best quality life. Our children's books are a key part of that mission, designed to promote growth and self-worth in young readers. Be sure to check out our website for tons of great blogs, resources, and even more amazing books. Let's work together to make a positive impact in our families and our communities!

In Health,
Kendrick, @TheEliteDad

We hope you enjoy the book, and would love for you to share your feedback and thoughts on our children's books by leaving a review.

www.blushchildren.com

Sign the Guestbook to receive updates for the next free ebook and video!

To all the amazing mothers, who have always been
rocks and sources of love and support.
This book is dedicated to you, with all my gratitude and love.
Thank you for loving and caring.

Most especially to my wife, Ashley.
- Kendrick, @TheEliteDad

Publisher's Cataloging-in-Publication data

Names: Monestime, Kendrick, author. | Berezina, Natalia, illustrator.
Title: Thank you , Mommy : heartfelt tribute of gratitude , appreciation , and celebration for
selfless mothers everywhere / by Kendrick Monestime; illustrated by Natalia Berezina.
Series: The Gratitude Series
Description: Erie, PA: BLUSH Children Books, 2023. | Summary: Children tell their mothers all
the things they are thankful for.
Identifiers: LCCN: 2023905713 | ISBN: 978-1-6851100-9-3 (hardcover) |
978-1-68511-024-6 (paperback) | 978-1-6851101-0-9 (ebook) | 978-1-6851101-1-6 (Kindle)
Subjects: LCSH Mothers--Juvenile literature. | Mother and child--Juvenile literature. | BISAC
JUVENILE NONFICTION / Family / Parents
Classification: LCC HQ759.M66 Th 2023 | DDC 306.874/3--dc23

# Thank You, Mommy

Written by
## Kendrick Monestime

Illustrated by
## Natalia Berezina

# Thank you, Mommy,

for giving me all of your love.
There's lots I love about
what you do for me.

# Thank you, Mommy,

for teaching me
to take care of my body.
When I am active,
I keep my body healthy.

# Thank you, Mommy,

for being by my side
when I'm trying something new.
You give me courage to explore
and give new things a shot.

# Thank you, Mommy,

for fixing my cuts and boo-boos.
Your kisses have superpowers
that help me get better faster.

# Thank you, Mommy,

for letting me know
it's OK to be scared sometimes.
You help me be stronger than my fears.

# Thank you, Mommy,

for helping me to be brave.
You remind me that I am strong and capable.
Now, I know there's nothing I can't do.

# Thank you, Mommy,

for being patient
when teaching me things.
You give me the time I need to learn.

# Thank you, Mommy,

for saying sorry when you make a mistake.
You show me that we all make mistakes,
and that's okay!

# Thank you, Mommy,

for helping me put money
in my piggy bank.

It's important to save money for items
we need and want later.

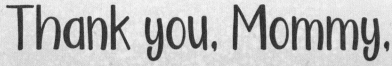

# Thank you, Mommy,

for showing me how to play while you are busy.
Playing by myself helps me
use my imagination and be creative.

# Thank you, Mommy,

for giving me food
that is good and tasty for me.
Healthy food helps me to become
smart and strong.

# Thank you, Mommy,

for bath time.
The toys and bubbles are fun,
and being super clean
keeps the germs away.

Thank you, Mommy,
for all the tickles, giggles,
and endless kisses.
Laughing with you makes me
feel happy and loved.

# Thank you, Mommy,

for reading me bedtime stories.
They take me on magical adventures
and help me have sweet dreams.

Thank you, Mommy,
for being so kind and loving.
Thank you for being

# MY EVERYTHING.

## About the Author

Founder of "Elite Dad", Kendrick Monestime is a passionate advocate for health and wellbeing. He has taken to various platforms, including his personal blog, Amazon, YouTube, podcasts, and Instagram, to inspire and motivate parents to lead healthy and fulfilling lives. Kendrick's love for wellbeing extends to spending as much time with his wife, two children, nieces, and nephews.

## About the Illustrator

Slovenian artist Natalia Berezina has illustrated more than 20 children's books, which are published in numerous countries all around the world. Natalia is a member of the Slovenian Association of Fine Art Societies. In addition to illustrating, she is passionate about acrylic painting on canvas, and her works have been featured in different exhibitions in Europe.

# More Books Coming Soon!

 **Thank You, Daddy**

 **Thank You, Grandpa**

**Thank You, Grandma**

**Thank You, Teacher**

Please leave a review by scanning the QR code or visting mothersdaybook.com

Made in the USA
Middletown, DE
26 April 2023

29468807R00020